TEARS IN THE BOTTLE of GRACE

The Journey of a Prodigal's Mom

Mari Madonna

All Scripture references are from the New American Standard Bible, 1995, published by the Lockman Foundation.

Copyright © 2016 Mari Madonna

All rights reserved.

ISBN-13: 9781519513625
ISBN-10: 1519513623

Put my tears in Thy Bottle;
Are they not in Thy book?

                         Ps 56:8

This is what the LORD says:
"Restrain your voice from weeping
And your eyes from tears;

for your work will be rewarded,"
declares the LORD.
"They will return from the land of the enemy.
So there is hope for your future,"
declares the LORD.

"Your children will return to their own land."

                         Jer. 31:16-17

**DEDICATED TO EACH OF YOU
WHO LOVE A PRODIGAL
AND
WAIT IN HOPEFUL
EXPECTANCY FOR THEM
TO COME HOME TO THE LORD.**

THANKS...

Where do I begin with thanks? There are so many people and situations that cause me to say thank you. First, it would have to be to my great LORD and King. He has been my great I AM, my deliverer, my rock my strength. He is the LORD who has known my name before there was time and gave me His Son to secure me eternally. His Spirit has guided my steps and given me the words for this book. For every situation and circumstance He has used to mold and shape me, I am forever grateful. Thank you, Abba Father.

For my Son, the greatest gift I have been given. I love him with all my heart and am so grateful the LORD gave him to me. He will always be someone I am proud of and treasure. For the family he loves which the LORD has given him. My granddaughters Charlotte and Corrine, words cannot express the joy that fills my heart to be a part of their lives and for the gift they are to me. Thank you. All my family and friends; the encouragement, the prayers, you have seen in me things I never could have. Thank you. For my precious sisters in the LORD, some old and lifelong, some new who I know pray for me without ceasing. You have been there for me again and again. Thank you.

For Deerfoot Lodge. There are no words to express the gratitude for all the years you invested into an eight-year-old boy, whose mother sent him to a wilderness boys camp his first year toting a suitcase, no hiking boots and white pants for banquet night! What did I know! For every Godly man who took time to show the love of God and live out a Godly example before him. For the dedication and the love and mentoring from that first year, to Guide, to Lone Eagle and most comforting now the promise to pray for him no matter what! Thank you.

For the "providential" traffic jam and the testimony of Jim Cymbala who was speaking of his daughter's days as a prodigal. It was that testimony the LORD used to begin Stand in the Gap, a prayer ministry for prodigals. For every person who faithfully came on Monday nights, month after month, and lifted up prayers of intercession for the prodigals entrusted to us. Thank you.

There are so many people who have helped to make this a book. Jan Silvious, who when I began to write Tears sat in my room so many years ago and encouraged me to tell my story. Thank you. Carolyn Capp, who gave me words of encouragement when I felt barren and could not write. Thank you. Debbie Barker, who took the time to read Tears when I first finished it putting commas and periods and words where they were needed. Thank you. For Tracey Jones, who took time from her own very busy world of writing and publishing to read Tears and then call me to encourage me to press on. Thank you. For Liz Scott, you are so very special always willing to go the extra mile. Thank you for proof reading it, the layout, and all you do to make publishing become real. For Arlene Pettersson, doing the finishing touches. Thank you. Carol Moye, another very unexpected gift. Only the LORD would take someone I had never met, who listened to me about a cover I imagined in my mind then prayed and designed exactly what was on my heart. Thank you. There are more I am sure who have encouraged me in prayer for this to come to pass. You know who you are. Thank you.

For my Mom who has been my ear, sitting and listening as I read to her everything I have written, whether it was an article, newsletter and now two books and at the end has always said, "Very nice." Thank you. And finally for my wonderful earthly Father, who is now rejoicing in Glory. You were a wonderful "Pop Pop," who took the time to make a little boy feel loved and valued. You made an impact in his life. Thank you.

Each of you is a gift, given to me, and to my great LORD I say, Thank you!

And THOUGHTS...

The style of this book is different. I am not a writer and really know nothing about the etiquette of writing. It is my style and mine alone. As you read you will see the name of the LORD always in capitals. It is how I write His name always. Using capitals reminds me always that His name is Holy and to be honored and revered. Whenever I write HE IS FAITHFUL, I write it in capitals, again reminding me He never has been anything less to me. You will never see me write satan with a capital. This may sound silly but in my mind he does not deserve the status of a proper noun.

And the BOOK...

This book is a book of encouragement. It is not like other books about prodigals. It is the story of my journey as the Mother of a prodigal. It is a story that has unfolded over many years. A story of being upheld in the loving and merciful arms of the LORD. It is a story in which the LORD has used His Word, prayer, others, and many situations to mold and shape me, teaching me through pain and many tears, "Things too wonderful for me, which I did not know." (Job 42:3) His arms have held me in His pinions and He has cradled me as He has gathered my tears in His never-ending bottle of Grace.

This book is written for each of you, who share in this journey; one none of us would have willingly chosen, yet the LORD in His wisdom has called us to enter in and travel. It is my hope that you will be encouraged as you read these pages. It is my hope too, that you will find your treasures in the darkness you face and that the LORD will give you Grace to face your journey. Along with my hope for you, is my prayer that you will be comforted in His Love.

In Christ,
Mari Madonna

CONTENTS

	DEDICATION	iv
	THANKS	v
1	FORESHADOWED GRACE	1
2	THE FIRST WEEK	4
3	THE VALLEY OF THE SHADOW OF DEATH	14
4	WHEN FRIENDS MEAN WELL	21
5	THE LONG JOURNEY: Treasures in the Darkness	31
6	SURRENDER	36
7	JEWELS OF GRACE: Standing on the Promises	44

1
FORESHADOWED GRACE

Looking back over the years I can see how the LORD goes before us, preparing us for the journeys we never would have willingly chosen on our own. Such is the case for me which began in the fall of 1998. I was at a ladies retreat, and the day could not have been more beautiful. We were instructed to go and read something from the Scripture and then return and share with the group. As I sat in the sun on that beautiful fall day, I could not have felt more at peace. The warm rusts and oranges filled the mountains in the background. The warmth of the sun filled me with such peace and joy as I took in the splendor of creation surrounding me. I remember being filled with both joy and a sense of blessing.

Not having any particular passage in mind, I turned to Isaiah 45 and began to read the chapter. When I finished reading, I could not stop thinking about verses two and three, ***"I will go before you and make the***

rough places smooth; I will shatter the doors of bronze and cut through their iron bars. I will give you treasures of darkness and hidden wealth of secret places. In order that you may know that it is I, The LORD, the God of Israel, who calls you by your name." (Italics and bold mine) I remember asking the LORD, "Why is this verse nagging at me? There are no rough places in my life."

If anything, I felt too blessed and questioned at times why my life did not have its share of hard places. Not that I was complaining, mind you, or asking the LORD to change the status of my comfort zone in any way, but the thought had crossed my mind from time to time. When discussions involving the topic of suffering came up, I felt removed and unable to completely relate to the struggles and suffering others encountered. In every respect, I believed my life was good and the lines for me had truly fallen in pleasant places. Over the years I have learned suffering and hard places take on many forms and my perception of suffering was naïve. Suffering in my mind equaled the martyrs of the Church, not the daily day-to-day routines of a hard working single mom.

I marked the date in my Bible, as I usually do when the Spirit speaks to my heart through the Word. That beautiful fall day the reading from the Scripture produced a tension within me and confused me. The wording was even strange, verse three was peculiar, "treasures of darkness" and "hidden wealth of secret places." The verses produced within me a sense of mystery, after all who can see in darkness and who finds anything hidden in secret places? I reflected some more and went to share with the ladies these two very peculiar verses the LORD had laid upon my heart. The LORD would take the principles of this ancient old prophecy of Cyrus, His anointed, during an appointed time in history to prepare His daughter by His grace for a time that was coming; just as He had done so long ago for the Nation of Israel.

Tucked within the pages of my Bible there was a note that would be a reminder for me in the years to come. Those puzzling "rough places" the LORD had touched me with on that beautiful autumn day were a beginning. He would teach His daughter. He would be my greatest "treasure" in my "darkest" moments. His abounding love and mercy would become my storehouses of "hidden wealth from His secret places." It would bring me to a place where I would meet my Father and cry out on my knees, broken, the tears at times inconsolable. He would meet me and those secret places would become my Jewels of Grace as His loving arms would hold His broken child. The journey was about to begin.

2
THE FIRST WEEK

This could not really be happening I thought as I listened to my son. "I don't want to be a Christian anymore." Not my son who had given his life to the LORD as a child, who had been taught the Scriptures and grown up in the faith. Not my son, who had grown up in the Church. This could not be happening.

Though not perfectly, it had been my desire to build our home upon the Word of God. I wanted him to understand the Scripture was the foundation his life needed to be built upon. I wanted him to know within its pages he would find the sound principles he would need to mold his character with integrity. There was no directive in my mind that made more sense than to train up my child in the LORD. The words of Deuteronomy 6:4-9 were the first verses we memorized together. His Word was to be ever before us. Ingrained upon our hearts were to be the commands of our God.

Some know the exact day and time they were saved and for others it is a progressive work in their lives. I know from childhood the LORD was actively involved in my life. After the birth of my son my desire to have faith began to grow once again. I wanted to know about the Bible. Around his third birthday the LORD began to draw me and finally I was faced with the same question Elijah asked the children of Israel on Mount Carmel. How long would I hesitate between two opinions? If what I was learning in the Scripture was true and it was, and Christ was indeed my Savior I could no longer sit on the fence embracing the world Monday through Saturday and pick up my Bible, dust it off on Sunday and play church. In 1984, I was ready to commit my life completely to the LORD. There would be no more hesitating between two opinions any longer. I wanted my talk and the walk to reflect the Savior who bore my sin and had set the captive free. And so it was for me, as it was for everyone who had gone before or would come after, the LORD began His transforming work in my life. Gradually He was removing from my life the entanglements that stood in the way of my life in Christ. Some entanglements were harder to leave behind, some easily discarded, but slowly and steadily the LORD was drawing me and replacing the old heart with a new one.

The work had been done and the transformation of my mind was in progress. As the LORD began to change my life, the truth of Scripture had a profound effect on all aspects of my life. No other book made the claims of Scripture, it was God's revelation to man. The

Scripture was completely able to transform the hearts and minds of men. It gave a clear description of how to be made right with a Holy and Righteous God.

Parenting took on a whole new dimension for me, and it became important to pass the truths of God's Word to my son. Scripture was not a philosophy or an all roads lead to God storybook. This book, called the Bible was different; the words were God-breathed words. As the truth of Scripture began to mold and shape my life the understanding of my role as a mother changed tremendously.

My Creator had entrusted me with a soul to care for and if I loved my son the implications of this truth had to weigh heavily upon me. I had been given a serious responsibility to teach my son the truths of Scripture and someday I would be called to give an account to the LORD on how I had handled that directive. How I lived my life before my son and what I taught him about Jesus mattered. The eternal worth of my son's soul was far too valuable to ignore. I could not neglect nor compromise the reality the LORD had given me. The Scripture would be the foundation within our home. The Word would be taught and lived: devotions, memory verses, Sunday school, morning and evening worship, brigade, youth group, and the opportunity for him to go to one of the finest boys Christian camps in the Northeast became the routine of our home.

As thoughts flooded my mind, I wanted to tell him he was mistaken, that he was just going through some delusional moment, to just think it through and it would all go away. I wanted to shake him, and perhaps he would come to his senses. *What I wanted?* I wanted to remind him he was the one who had wanted Jesus in his heart; he was the one who had talked so many times of going on the mission field. Whose Bible did I pick up with underlined verses everywhere? Who had picked only one college to go to that was a Christian one? Who wrote all those letters I have tucked away that spoke of a personal walk of faith? My decision for *you*? My mind was racing with memories of conversations, of moments we had shared in the LORD. Surely he had to understand the absolute confusion in his statement.

But I knew my son too, and his history, the years that were his background and all the Christian influences that had molded his life. He was well grounded and rooted in his Christianity. He was not one to make rash decisions and thought things through, counting the cost in the areas of concern that were a part of his life. There was no doubt in my mind that his decision now was not any different. I had seen the struggles begin, had watched him wrestle with issues surrounding his faith, never really thinking they were strong enough for him to leave Christ. I had been both a silent and verbal observer in his journey of faith; there was no doubt as he sat there and disowned the faith he had once so seriously embraced that he was saved. Now God would teach me that He was the Faithful One. He would be the Father who does not lie.

Although I knew these truths, the reality of this moment was one I could not grasp and one I did not want to believe for a moment. This young man sitting across from me whom I loved so dearly was telling me the truth; he was leaving his walk with the LORD. I knew better than to say all that flooded my mind and so we talked. We had one of the many heart-to-hearts that had molded our many years as mother and son. In that talk was the discussion of the sad reality we would face as time went on. We discussed the truths that every parent is faced with when their child makes the decision to leave their faith.

We were no exception. We talked about our views and how they would now be approached from two very different perspectives. I reminded him that I would still be the Christian mother who made her decisions based on the Word of God. There would be situations that we would face from different world views and values and those situations would be the potential for strife between us as we saw them from totally different perspectives. It was a difficult conversation between mother and son and we both cried at one point. I felt a helplessness that was indescribable and the sadness that was invading my heart was unbearable.

This was my son, the gift from God to me. How could it be? How could he walk away from his Savior? He knew Jesus. Jesus had made a mark on his life, one that was a serious mark and now he would walk away? I wanted to remind him of the words of Solomon, to remember the God of his youth. I wanted to tell him that his life without Christ at the center would be meaningless, that his times would get difficult, that his decisions would be made with wrong motives and that his choices could have serious consequences. I wanted to go on and on with all the principles that come from a walk of faith and the wisdom that is found in His Word.

Yet there was nothing I could tell him that he did not know or understand. He had grown up in the faith and understood the principles that direct a walk of faith. What I did was to encourage him of my love and to promise him I would pray for him. I followed up with a note to him. I asked that he would remember his words to me as we had talked about wisdom riding on a train to New York. That day I expressed my thoughts to him and made a statement to him about what I believed wisdom was. He was quick to point out to me my theology was not correct. He pointed out to me the fear of the LORD was the beginning of all wisdom and I stood corrected. His point was indeed correct. I remember thinking that this was all a dream and I would wake up and none of this sadness would be real. But it was real, very real.

So much of that first week as I look back felt surreal. I had a hollow in my heart and a sadness that would not budge. I am amazed how the LORD immediately came alongside of me cradling the hurting heart I had. I cried out many, many times to Him in that first week and He lovingly was there.

I was reading through the Bible in a year and it 'just so happened' during my devotion time that first week, I read from 2 Chronicles 20. The tears welled in my eyes, this passage of Scripture throughout the years was an anchor of hope for me—but that day and at that moment the LORD was using it as a place of refuge to comfort me.

It is a familiar text of Scripture, Jehoshaphat is faced with a great battle and it looks so hopeless. The big boys are coming and Jehoshaphat is scared. I knew the story. I had read it so many times, and many of the verses the LORD had used to touch my heart were underlined. Through the years I had come to this passage over and over when I needed to understand His power, His might and when I needed to find comfort in the magnitude of the God I could rest in because of His love for me.

Today was different. I had not sought out this passage, and He in Grace had led me to it knowing it would be my lifeline of hope and encouragement. He met me in the pages of His Word and spoke to my heart in an instant, comforting me as only He could. I read on, the familiar story—Jehoshaphat coming before the LORD, Jehoshaphat declaring a fast in Judah and an assembly, reminding God of His awesome character and power and his utter hopelessness before his mighty LORD in the situation he was facing. The words of Jehoshaphat I knew so well, "We don't know what to do but our eyes are upon You." That was me that day. The battle was a big one, too big for me and I, like

Jehoshaphat, was saying the very same thing LORD, "It's too big. I haven't a clue. I am scared and feeling so overwhelmed, but LORD I am looking right at you. I can't go anywhere else."

The story continues, the Bible says that right there in the midst of the nation, God by His Spirit, meets with the people through Jahaziel and proclaims to the nation, "The battle is not yours." Just as He declares, He fights the battle and even goes one step further and tells the nation don't do a thing—just stand there. "See the salvation of the LORD on your behalf." (2 Chr. 20:17) Just as He declares the LORD fights the battle and the victory is won.

This wonderful text of Scripture took on new meaning for me that day. This was the Scripture that had always been my hope for those I loved who were not saved, but today the LORD was using it in a different way to comfort my hurting heart. The LORD had spoken, it was not my battle, I could do nothing. It was too great a battle and I was not equipped to do what the LORD could do better. The tears rolled down my face. The battle would be the LORD's and the victory would be His too. The months to come would teach me over and over this fundamental principle that He had revealed to me this day. This was not my battle, it was His. I had two things to remember within the chapter, one: was to pray and two: was to station myself in trustful expectancy.

The days passed and the LORD kept touching me and holding me. There were so many emotions I dealt with in that first week. There was an emptiness that was ever present and a hollowness that did not leave. I felt as if I were in a fog that would not lift and at times the pain that tore at my heart made me want to cry out.

God remained my shield and my buckler. I can still recall the utter hopelessness that shrouded me and remember how His tender mercy took His hurting child and lovingly embraced her. He cradled my heart and gave me hope in my wilderness comforting me with His tenderness. Soon after, I was reading Romans 8 and once again I was touched by the awesome assurance of the LORD. For every Christian, Romans 8 is a treasure chest ranging from deep doctrinal truth, to words of comfort and eternal assurance. It begins with the assurance of eternal security for the believer and ends with the infallible truth of contrasting merism used to solidify that there is nothing that is able to separate us from Him.

I read the chapter, each thought building upon the next, truth following truth, and when I came to verse 29, once again the Spirit of God moved me. "For those whom He foreknew, He also predestined to become conformed to the image of His Son." (Rom 8:29) Again I stood amazed at the wonder of the God who knew me and was inclined to the cry of His child. He is the One who knows our pain and hears our laments. My God, my LORD holding me and making me aware of His promise. The promise of God in Christ for every believer. There on the pages of His Holy Word, He was giving comfort to my grieving heart, letting me know that the promises of God are yea and amen. The truth of the text said one thing loud and clear, the promise of God is: to conform every believer to the image of His Son—it is the promise of God, not man and that is binding. It transcends the circumstances of the sinner; it is cemented in the nature and character of a God that cannot lie.

My heart leaped with joy as I read the promise of my God to me that day. My God promised to conform my prodigal son to the image of His Son. To make him into a picture of the Savior he had professed. Truth; not according to my understanding, but according to the God who cannot lie. The verse gave no time frame, only the outcome of the promise of God. I knew not the when. I only knew that day for a mother hurting for her son there was a promise from the God who held my prodigal son's life in His hands. There would be a time when he would be conformed to the image of God's own Son. I marked my Bible with my son's initials and the year; 1999. God had spoken and it would come to pass.

3
THE VALLEY OF THE SHADOW OF DEATH

My son was the greatest blessing in my life. As a young child he did not have a great deal of interaction with his father. We had our share of challenges and dealt with situations that made life difficult at times. I am sure the situations I faced as a single mother parallels many other single mothers who are both mother and father to their child and equally not prepared for such a role. My son was an exceptional child, truly an amazing young boy who grew into a wonderful teenager and then young adult. I never experienced the dreaded rebellion of the teen years so many parents experience. We shared a special closeness from his childhood into his college years. I have so many cherished memories of his growing years.

Children need to feel they belong and are not different or odd. They need to feel the security which comes from feelings of acceptance and belonging. When that security is threatened due to any situation, they are left sorting out the confusion they may not be prepared to handle.

When I raised my son, for a period of time we were the only single-parent family in our church that was the result of a divorce. What I did not understand and learned much too late is: a child growing up within the church, who comes from a single parent home, regardless of the cause, faces hurdles that can be difficult for them.

My son did not have the 'normal' two-parent home which for the most part was the norm that surrounded him in our church. I believe I may have missed situations that may have been sensitive for him to deal with and had I understood I could have helped to sort out some of the issues that he was faced with. Sadly, now for a child to come from a divorced home is more common within the church than ever before and there are many support groups to help in the dynamic of single parenting. I feel I learned too late the emotional burdens that children face coming from single-parent homes.

Despite that sad fact, from the time he was four our lives circled around the activities of life within our church family. The LORD used my son in many ways to change my heart. I was newly getting back into going to church and not totally committed in my walk with the LORD. I did not think reading the Bible would change me or my life. Initially, what drew me was curiosity. I wanted to know why the Bible was different from other world views. It claimed to be a book filled with the truth of God and if that was the case I wanted to see what it had to say.

One thing I was convicted of and resolute about was my child needed to go to church. The reason for this conviction was not at all clear to me. It was more the sense of moral conviction than commitment to the things of the LORD at that time. Since I was his mother I had the responsibility to church my child!

So, I picked up the Bible and we read and together we learned. The LORD had a different plan and the seeds of His truth were being planted and those seeds began to touch my heart and convict me. I needed to live the faith I professed and there could be no more room for wavering between two opinions. That moment of conviction became also the moment of transformation and a journey began. The WORD, the inerrant WORD of God's Truth became the foundation upon how our home would be built. The purpose of our home would be fixed upon the things of the LORD. As I look back now, I am humbled at how the LORD proved Himself FAITHFUL by His patience and love. The years that have followed have been the sweetest years as He has molded me, shaped me and convicted me.

During those years He taught me how to be a mother and how to love my son. He taught me the value of the responsibility He had given me in being a parent and how high a priority it was to be in my life. He taught me how to stand upon His Word and that my life before my son was to be lived by example.

We faced our share of difficult times in those years. Money was tight, and living space cramped but we had each other. I worked my way through school and became a nurse. We learned what it meant to use our time wisely and to make the most of it. We went bicycle riding or ate out at our favorite fast food place, Wendy's. We played games at home or rented movies and watched them. We went on camping trips, cheap vacations, and found many kinds of activities to do. My son loved to swim and play miniature golf. At eight years old, he started to go to Deerfoot Lodge, a Christian boys camp in the wilderness of the Adirondack Mountains. It would be the single most important event in his life until he was 19 years old.

My son had wonderful grandparents. Although both took active rolls in helping to raise him, it was the father figure of his "Pop Pop" that made an impact on his life. Both my parents were a picture of sacrificial love, caring for their grandchild while I worked and went to school. I owe them a debt I can never repay for all of their sacrifice. The years went by and in 1996, my son left for Messiah College. Never would I have anticipated in three short years our lives would change and I would feel a distance from the son I loved so much.

The months that followed my son's decision to walk away from the LORD were filled with darkness and fear for me. We had a distance between us now I was not used to and arguments were almost a part of our every conversation or visit. Truly it was a time of darkness for me and I felt I was in the valley of the shadow of death.

I felt my son slipping from me as the distance grew between us and sadness filled my heart. My cry to the LORD was the cry of Psalm 34:18; a cry of a broken heartedness that only He could understand.

There were times I did not hear from him and I was filled with anxiety and concern. When we did speak, at times he seemed okay, other days I feared, not certain he was doing okay at all. For the first time in my life I experienced a sense of despair and hopelessness that was indescribable. It was hard to understand the transformation that I was witnessing in the life of my son in those early days as a prodigal. The confident son I had was filled with so much confusion. In the times of silence I was filled with so much fear. During that time my son left school and did not return for a year. So many times in the depths of despair I asked the LORD, "What are you doing?" "Why are you allowing this?" My emotions filled me and I could not believe that any of this was really real.

As I look back now the feeling of the shadow of death which seemed to surround me was to become a beginning for the mountain I needed to climb of surrender. The LORD was taking the hands that held on so tight and prying the fingers open one-by-one. My son was gone and the LORD was asking me in every painful moment, "Do you trust Me? Will you let him go? Or are you going to hold on tight?"

Every ounce of my strength shouted out to God, "You gave him to me, he is *my* son." "How could you let this happen? How could the son that I offered to you as a boy - like Hannah, how could you let it go this way?" "What kind of a God does this?"

In that moment of my deepest pain the reality of what I was screaming out to God became the beginning of surrender. My words brought me face-to-face with the truth of Divine reality. The story of Hannah offering her son Samuel back to the LORD had so moved me. I too had offered my son to the LORD. I had given him to the LORD in the same way Hannah gave Samuel to the LORD. There was not a temple I had taken him to and left him at, but my desires for him were the same as Hannah's for Samuel. I wanted my son to know his LORD, to serve Him, to hear His LORD speak to him and for him to listen.

The reality of this truth gripped my heart with such yearning, and yet there were many more moments of pain and fear I went through. Nonetheless, I had given my son to the LORD, just like Hannah. Unlike Hannah however, I had not come to the place of understanding that he was not mine. He was the LORD's. With the gentle touch of my own heavenly Father the reality became clear. I began to open the clenched fists that held tight to the son that was not mine; to let go of situations that I could not control. My fingers opened one-by-one, letting go of the son I had offered to the LORD so many years before. This time the hands were opened in the shape of surrender.

4
WHEN FRIENDS MEAN WELL

There are many emotions loved ones of prodigals go through. They vary anywhere from confusion, anger, pain, and guilt. Feelings of helplessness can overwhelm us at many times. During the early months of this new journey I went through a range of different emotions. At times there were feelings of sadness that would fill my day and I cried out to the LORD like the Psalmist, "How long, Oh, LORD?"

I blamed myself and questioned how I had failed? What had I missed with regard to the spiritual responsibility of raising my son? Was there an area I had overlooked or a command I had neglected? During those early months as I anguished in this abyss of questions and doubts there seemed to be no answers given me. I felt I had failed as a Christian parent and was completely inadequate. It was difficult to think others would see me in this light as well. We are so vulnerable and human in moments like this and each of us goes down the slippery slopes of wondering how this looks to those around us.

None of us want to look as if we have failed, especially when it comes to our children. I felt so unworthy in the light of other parents whose children were growing in their walk with the LORD. How painful it was, as the months turned to years and the children that my son had grown up with came to church and I watched them engaging in church life. I was the mother of a prodigal; certainly I had done something wrong which was the cause of his decision. Guilt plagued me too. Was I too legalistic, with a million rules that were not backed by the love of the LORD? Did I live by example before my son? Was I a hypocrite, who talked the talk but did not live the walk? I blamed and tormented myself relentlessly.

At times the emotions would switch, and I was like the brute beast of Psalm 73 embittered and filled with anger towards the LORD. In those ignorant moments I would demand the LORD to give me answers, explanations and shook my fists at the Almighty barraging Him with one question after another, "*How* could you allow this LORD?" "*Why* would you allow this?" "Is this how you repay faithfulness?" "What kind of God are *You*?" "What were all the years of faithful obedience for?" "Wasn't it Your instruction to teach my son Your Word and to make the Scriptures the directives to guide his life?" I had done it, diligently and faithfully and this was the reward of my labor? *Really*? I wanted to scream at the LORD for the way I felt He had handled my circumstances. I wanted to ask Him, "Why did I even bother?" If this was the end result, my reward, why had I even bothered? It was just a waste of time and all in vain.

In those moments of anger my heart was overwhelmed with a sadness that seemed inconsolable. I pleaded for answers, begging for my son to come home and my tears at times seemed to have no end. My son was a prodigal and we were going down roads I had never envisioned nor would have dreamed would have borne our name.

I blamed God, struggling to make sense of my confusion. At times I convinced myself that none of what was happening was real. I denied any of it was true, until the next situation would occur, and the reality would again set in motion another painful roller coaster of emotions.

How true were the words of Isaiah! The rough places had set in and darkness surrounded me. I felt I could not see the light any longer; my valley experience was an abyss of darkness. I no longer knew how to communicate with my son. It seemed each time we spoke a new battle would break out. Soon the phone calls became less and less frequent. Eventually our visits also became less and less and my heart was overwhelmed with grief.

The son I had been so close with slipped further and further from me. I mourned for the loss of our closeness, and yet I did not know how to bridge the gap between us. My Christianity became more and more offensive, and I did not know how to resolve the offensiveness it brought my son. We argued and politely ignored one another and over time the distance grew between us. Those moments were some of the most painful I think I have ever faced.

I believe the LORD used those months to let me accept the reality that my son's decision was real. It was another treasure in my journey through this darkness to allow me to understand it was me who needed to change. I was at a loss how any of what I was being convicted of would be accomplished, but I was sure that if I wanted a relationship with my son to survive, there was no other choice.

I was not my son's Holy Spirit and I could not change his heart or his decision. I was harassing my son at every turn, thinking I had the words to convict him and redirect him back to the LORD. The only thing I was accomplishing was creating a wall which grew higher and higher after each confrontation. There was nothing I could do. I needed to do some repenting myself.

If things were not bad enough in the midst of my Job experience, my very own Eliphaz, Bildad, and Zophar came to offer their insight and solutions to resolve the situation. Friends who meant well I am sure, but at times I wanted to scream like Job, "How long will you torment me and crush me with your words?" (Job 19:2) It would pierce my heart when I would hear the words, "Maybe your son is not saved." I would cry out to the LORD begging Him to console me. "Not saved, could that be?" I began to doubt and question and the agony tore at my heart. Could it be they were right? I begged the LORD to give me an answer and hold my hurting heart in His hand. "Please LORD this can't be so. I know that my son committed his life to you." Their words pierced me, and I could not get them out of my mind. Looking back now, I can understand their words were spoken out of concern. Such contrast exists in the life of a person who no longer lives as a believer. Many did not know my son and so they questioned. Those closest to him and me, however, never questioned his commitment to the LORD.

As I sought the LORD to settle my heart and to assure me of my son's eternal security, the LORD answered me again from the truth of His Word. It came over time, a time of beseeching Him and much prayer, but it came. The LORD began to use the life of Solomon to give me the answer I needed.

Solomon, the wisest of all the kings of the nation of Israel, lived most of his life as a prodigal. I am not sure many would see him as a prodigal but reading the book of Kings and Ecclesiastes made it clear to me. Although he knew the LORD, he did not honor Him or live a life committed to Him. In the final chapter of the book of Ecclesiastes we hear the cry of a king who had done everything under the sun and came up short every time only to declare the futility of an empty life. It was all vanity and striving after the wind. There was an emptiness in the life of Solomon as he had pursued every delight life had to offer. It was only at the end of his life that he came to understand his life of emptiness living apart from the LORD.

In Chapter 12, he laments and admonishes his readers to "remember the God of your youth." It took Solomon an entire lifetime to finally understand the most important need in his life and the answer for life was to know God, keep His commandments and fear Him. The wisest man who ever lived had missed the mark! He had blown it, totally and completely. As the king he was to represent Yahweh to the Nation. Instead, he married pagan wives, built temples for them and offered sacrifices to their gods. Solomon, elected by the LORD, had blown it. His final moments show clearly his understanding that he had failed to remember the LORD who had appeared to him twice. The writer of Kings declares, "His heart was not wholly devoted to the LORD." (1 Kings 11:4) He denied himself no pleasure, lived his life as a pagan and ran after the things that never fulfilled him as His God could have. Page after page Ecclesiastes describes the man Solomon who had forgotten the God of his youth. He had forsaken Him for the vanities of this life which left him chasing after the wind. The prodigal King, a prodigal life!

I also began to think of time. How short our lives are here on this earth. Psalm 90 describes the fleeting moments of our lives, finishing them with a sigh, gone all so soon. We are told to number our days. The LORD has created us to exist within the boundaries of time, yet within our finite minds we cannot fully comprehend time.

Important guidelines are created using time as a reference point to structure day-to-day activities. We evaluate situations and circumstances using the reference of time to draw conclusions. The reality in which we exist is interwoven within this phenomenon called time. It is a tool designed for our lives that gives us a sense of ordered structure and balanced priorities. Days, weeks, months, years, these fragments make up the existence of what the Bible calls the span of our lives. Man is dependent on time and could not function in life without it.

Not so with the LORD. He is not dependent on time. He does not live within the boundaries of time nor is He limited by it or contained within it. He has established time for us but has no need of it. There is no measure of time within the realm of eternity. It has no beginning or end. In attempting to understand these concepts the only thing we truly accomplish is to get more lost within them. The Bible gives us a glimpse in the depth of this great mystery "with the LORD one day is like a thousand years and a thousand years like one day." (2 Peter 3:8)

As I thought about the life of Solomon and the mystery of time the LORD allowed me to understand more fully His promise of eternal life. How I evaluate my world can only be understood within my limited understanding of time. When months turn to years for someone who walks away from the LORD it is understandable for them to be seen as never having been saved at all. What I believe the LORD needed to teach me was time with regard to eternity bears no significance in the life of a prodigal. Although I understood that the length of time a person is a prodigal is meaningless in the realm of eternity, I also understood the seriousness of living away from the LORD.

The LORD is merciful, gracious and long-suffering. His desire is for repentance and reconciliation always. Grieving and quenching the Spirit of the living God is a serious thing with serious consequences. Throughout the Scripture are continual warnings for those who transgress the Holiness of God and His commands. It is not a matter to be taken lightly. The Proverbs continually give warning of not being attentive to the wisdom the LORD offers. It begins with a wise man having understanding, hearing and acquiring sound instruction, and it ends with a woman of virtue filled with wisdom and admired by all who know her. What begins with Chapter 1 and ends with Chapter 31 is the theme of the entire book allowing men and women access to this wisdom is one statement, "the Fear of the LORD." (Pr. 1:7, Pr. 31:30) It is the glue, the mortar of all things necessary in this life.

Likewise are the admonishments to those who choose the opposite. Sobering and frightening warnings can also be found in Proverbs. Chapter 1:24-33, the LORD makes it clear the outcome of those who refuse His out stretched hand or His call. Continued disobedience leaves no other option God can offer to them, but there will be no answer for them. They will not find Him. The why is evident within the Scripture, they refused Him and they would not turn to Him. Chapter 5 describes being held in the captivity of sinfulness and folly. Chapter 11, verse after verse describes the contrast of the righteous and the wicked. Chapter after chapter is filled with those who despise the Word of God, forsaking the way of God. Proverbs 28:14 so clearly states, "He who hardens his heart falls into calamity."

These verses fill my heart with sadness. The Spirit of the Living God can be grieved into silence. We are allowed to live lives separated from Him and the reason for our creation—relationship with Him. How tragically sad. I have often wondered what that moment had to be like when Peter saw Jesus turn and look at him after he had denied Him. I cannot even imagine, but can only guess the moment had to be filled with intense anguish and sorrow. I also wonder if that will not be the same experience for those who choose to live apart from the One they had confessed to love and be committed to.

But God... I love those words! They are two of the greatest words in the Scripture. Hope can also be found in the pages of Proverbs. Proverbs 16: 6 is one of those verses. "By lovingkindness and truth iniquity is atoned for, and by the fear of the LORD one keeps away from evil." How true is that verse? God's lovingkindness brings us hope.

Loving-kindness ~ hesed ~ is a covenantal word in the Old Testament, and the LORD is a God of covenant. He does not forsake His covenant nor does He forsake those who have given themselves to Him at the moment of their salvation. The One who begins the work is also the One who completes it. His promise is not limited by time for His atoning work was before there was time.

This LORD of covenant was the One who called my son from darkness to light and allowed him to share in the inheritance of the saints. It was done at Calvary, finished and completed when my son asked Jesus to be his Savior. This same Savior would never leave him nor forsake him, no matter how long the segment of time would be. His LORD had finished the work on the tree, every sin covered, none left without His knowledge, none, unable to forgive.

I needed to trust and believe in the truth of His Word. The finished work of redemption was accomplished outside of time and apart from human comprehension. It was complete and secured only within a Sinless Savior.

5

THE LONG JOURNEY:
Treasures In The Darkness

The days moved onward as my son kept his distance and I kept mine. The Scripture, prayer and knowing the LORD was my anchor amidst this storm keeping me focused and pressing on. The reality had imbedded itself within me. I was the mother of a prodigal. Although I was foreign to this new role and resented it, I needed to move forward. Questions continually came to my mind. What would we talk about? What about Church? What about his dating choices? How was I to be a godly mother to a son who did not desire godly things? It all seemed absurd as I thought and thought, the issues going round and round. No longer did I hide behind the pretense it would all go away and our Christian home would be as it was before that day in June. It was real. My son was in the world and I was in the LORD.

The confrontation between us continued at times or even worse the dreaded distance. I felt we had a thick dense wall that kept us more and more separated. At times the arguments seemed as if we were at war and it was impossible to find common ground. The reality of the conversation on that June day so long ago became more and more evident. We were in two different worlds, separated by a gulf of divided walks. The words of Jesus true, we were a divided house.

It seemed incredible that this was the relationship I now shared with my son. We had shared a special closeness and so many wonderful conversations. This was the same son who once had told me how much it meant to him to see his mother with her Bible in her hands doing her devotions, yet now was angered by the things that had been a part of our everyday lives. This new normal was the fuel to fan the fire of anger and harsh words. I did not know what to do or what to say. The cards with verses I sent became cards that caused arguments and my "God bless you," were words to be silenced. The conversations about the LORD, once spoken so freely were now areas of contention. The truth of the Word became a battleground of self-righteous religion. What my son had once embraced no longer had credibility and was not to be discussed.

I must confess I did not handle those days well. I continually came to the places I thought I had done so well in only to feel I was losing ground and falling flat on my face. The same situations resurfaced and the same lessons seemed to come full circle needing to be relearned. I was confrontational and often harsh with my son. I argued with him and fought with him as if it was my duty to win the war. I was determined to fight the battle and even more so I was determined to win. This was *my* son and I was *his* mother and there was no way that I was about to let this war end without the victory being mine! It became very clear however, as time moved forward, that this war had a loser and it was me. I would not only lose the battle but I would lose my son in the process. I needed to change my own self-righteous attitude.

The LORD was long-suffering with me time after time as He showed His compassion to my frame made of dust. The LORD, through His Spirit, again gave me His treasures in the darkness of that fall day that seemed ages ago. The battle was not mine. His Word would allow me to be comforted and still. The lessons from His secret place were the same, that of continued surrender, to let go of what was only possible with Him.

His Word gave me the strength to go forward, holding on to every promise He poured out upon me, my treasures, my strength and my strong tower. This was the LORD who had formed my son in the womb, who knew him when he was formed in the secret place. He was the Sovereign LORD that held this rebel child in His loving arms. My son was my gift from the LORD, entrusted to me but ultimately He was the lover of his soul. He alone knew what would work best in his life.

I began to mark each time the LORD touched me and assured me with a treasure in my dark and overcast world. Little by little they became my treasures, my Jewels of Grace, His Grace, bringing a light in the midst of my darkness. The LORD was the FAITHFUL God of promise and the lessons of letting go were not easy but I needed each one.

It was while my son was visiting home that the LORD touched me with a special treasure and was about to teach me a valuable lesson. I was doing my devotion and was in the book of Habakkuk. This prophet to the Southern Kingdom had some questions himself regarding the wickedness that was out of control in Judah. I could relate, I had some questions of my own and I had no problem with bringing them to the LORD either. There were many times the questions I had were not asked in a manner pleasing to the LORD in any way. It seemed that Habakkuk was singing my tune as he asked the LORD, "How long, O LORD will I call for help and you will not hear?" (Hab. 1:2) Didn't the LORD care? Habakkuk was not very pleased with what was going on in Judah and where was the LORD anyway? Why wasn't He doing anything about all the evil that was going on? He was the LORD, wasn't He? And shouldn't He be jumping at Habakkuk's snapping fingers, and mine? It sounded logical to me!

"LORD I have a prodigal here, I've been praying and fasting and time is marching on. Why aren't you doing anything? Where are you?" And just as the LORD answered Habakkuk, He was about to answer me.

The LORD's answer to Habakkuk was His answer for me also. "Look among the nations! Observe! Be astonished! Wonder! Because I am doing something in your days—You would not believe if you were told." (Hab. 1:5)

It was time for me to keep quiet. It was time to observe that my great LORD had it all under control and was working out all the details according to His plan. It was not my job to question the plan or demand answers to what was none of my business.

I can still remember the smile that came upon my face that day. More treasures I could hold onto, I got the message! My LORD was going to do something; something that would be astonishing and even more importantly—He didn't need to tell me!

6
SURRENDER

The much needed change began, sometimes it would be with great strides and at other times I felt I was back at ground zero. In those moments when it seemed my frustration and weariness would come again from rehashing the same questions of the past the LORD remained FAITHFUL. Transformation was coming, slowly but steadily. Situations still occurred and my heart still grieved. The hurt seemed more painful when I saw friends whose children were serving and walking with the LORD. The times I returned to Deerfoot were difficult. It was a place filled with so many memories. The impact it had made on my son and the many memories which seemed to be everywhere made it difficult and bitter-sweet. The question always lingered in the back of my mind, how anyone touched to the depth my son had been at Deerfoot could just turn and ignore all the truth he had embraced. It made no sense to me and I wanted so badly to comprehend all my unanswered questions.

During these steps back I wanted the LORD to fix everything and make it go away. I was like the writer of Psalm 73, running a close second and at times maybe even trying hard for first place! My heart was pierced within and I was senseless and ignorant too. I wanted answers; I wanted change; I wanted to see it over and done. I was crying out to the LORD begging for it to come to pass and NOTHING. No changes, everything remained status quo.

Just as Asaph pondered all he was facing, I did the same too. The difference however, was Asaph went into the sanctuary of the LORD. When he did that he was able to find answers and see more clearly. The Spirit of the LORD was again ready to give me another needed step in the journey. I needed to step into the sanctuary of His Word and into the sanctuary of prayer so I could meditate and find the answers too. One lesson at a time, I was being given the opportunity to frequent His sanctuary.

I confess it was not really what I wanted to do at times, but His sanctuary humbled me and my fingers opened one at a time. Each time the rewards were treasures to fill the hands I opened upward towards Him. My prayers became filled with desire for Him to fill me, for surrender to be one moment at a time and for me to move closer and closer to Him. Each secret place where I learned the treasures He gave me was marked in my Bible. They were there so I would not forget this journey, one that was of stumbling and falling but of getting up and holding onto a FAITHFUL God who knew me. His Word became my strength; He was upholding His daughter in His mighty hands.

One year, on Mother's Day I visited a church that was giving out a devotional booklet called, <u>Parents on Their Knees</u>, by Vi Goodrich. Every verse used in the booklet I looked up and wrote in my devotional. I did not want to miss any of the treasures within this booklet. It was food for my soul. The very last devotional dealt with the prodigal. As I read that day, I shared with a woman I had never met, her cries were mine also. Jeremiah 31:16-17 touched my heart, filling my eyes with tears.

The LORD used those two verses, and they have become the anchor of hope I hold onto in hopeful expectancy for the future I trust will come to pass. In my Bible, forever etched on the page of Jeremiah 31:16-17, I have written, "Thank you dear Father, I wait in expectancy."

The passage deals with Rachel weeping for her children and refusing to be comforted. Verses 16 and 17 read, Thus says the LORD, "Restrain your voice from weeping and your eyes from tears; for your work shall be rewarded," declares the LORD, "And *they shall return* from the land of the enemy. There is hope for your future," declares the LORD, "And *your children shall return* to their own territory." (italics mine)

There in the Word, the LORD placed His comforting hand upon the heart of His daughter gently assuring me. Two different women, at two different moments in history, the situations very different, but the truth very much the same; the God who offered comfort then and now was the same and He was very much in control.

He loved this wayward prodigal. All the years of raising him, teaching him, instructing him in the ways of the LORD would not be in vain. My tears would be dried and the comfort that seemed fleeting at times was sure. There was a great LORD telling me to be still, to trust. He had the power to return my prodigal from the land of the enemy, a land that he did not belong to. He would return him to the land he truly belonged to.

Once again there was no mention of time. There was only a promise for me in the pages of His Word that day. I could trust the LORD and be certain a day of deliverance was coming, a day to be comforted, a day when tears would be wrapped in the joy of a son who would be restored to the territory of the LORD he truly belonged to. I could hope in the LORD I knew.

Once again the LORD filled my brokenness. He was my LORD of promise. He was molding me to trust Him beyond what I could only see. He was using my prodigal son and the crucibles of fire removing the dross that filled his daughter's heart. With each new situation He was allowing His Word to transform me and mold me and shape me. Each tear, each day of despair began to be used to transform me into a trophy of His Grace.

My knees became my refuge to fall to, and His Word became the stronghold that held me tight.

In the summer of 2003 I was to return to Deerfoot Lodge. The memories of Deerfoot were imbedded into my soul from his first summer as a camper, one memory following another, to the year he was picked for his guide summer at 16, to staff and finally to the honor of Lone Eagle. I had not been there in a few years and now was going back to volunteer. I can remember the apprehension I felt in the weeks prior to leaving for camp. I wondered if I had made the right decision and how would I handle all the memories that always inundated me while I was there? Anxiety began to take hold of me.

I was to leave on Saturday morning and my heart was filled with heaviness. I was reading the book of Isaiah and my text for that day was Isaiah 59. How many times have we read the Scripture and we read a verse and it is as if we have read it for the first time and it moves us? Isaiah 59 begins with that familiar verse of His hand not being short that He cannot save or His ear dull that He cannot hear. A good word from the LORD who knew the circumstances and was fully equipped to deal with the situation at hand. I read on. The all too familiar picture was painted again regarding the sin of God's people. They were truly a rebellious nation. God was displeased. He, by His own strength, would bring about the needed salvation and restoration for the Nation.

The salvation He described of course would be ushered in by the LORD Himself in the person of His Son. A Redeemer would come to Zion. It was verse 21 that caught my eye that morning. "As for Me, this is My covenant with them," says the LORD, "My Spirit which is upon you, and My words which I have put in your mouth shall not depart from your mouth, nor from the mouth of your offspring, nor the mouth of your offspring's offspring," says the LORD, "from now and forever more."

I could not believe what my eyes were reading and the timing could not have been more perfect. The LORD who had given hope to a rebellious Nation unable to save themselves from their sinfulness was confirming the same thing to me. The Nation of Israel was a stiff-necked people. Over and over again the LORD was the FAITHFUL provider to them despite their rebellious hearts. The sins of the Nation angered Him to the very core. I am always amazed when, within the Scripture; over and over again we read those words: But God. As I read that day in Isaiah 59:21 there was a But God in the form of covenant. The LORD is the God of covenant, initiated by Him and kept by Him unable to ever be broken. In the garden the LORD set in motion a covenant of promise that would come in the fullness of time. The theme of that covenant is the story of redemptive history. The pages of Isaiah are filled with the theme of a covenant keeping God.

Verse 21, was clear, the promise of the covenant of the LORD would not fail. His Spirit and the words He gave and put into the mouth of His children would not depart. His covenant was not to be taken lightly. It was the covenant of promise that extended not only for the Nation, but for generations of believers. It could not be violated, rejected or maligned. It was a covenant sealed by the blood of a Savior.

How precious a truth the LORD had laid upon my heart that morning. I had been touched by the great I AM and there was rest for my soul. I had the assurance I needed. There was a promise of hope that filled my needy heart. The reassured promise from the covenant initiator and keeper were the words that had been taught to my son from his youth. They were the words of the LORD Himself. They were words of truth. He was the One who alone could save and for all those who put their hope in Him, they would not be ashamed. This was the LORD of the covenant who showed me He would be FAITHFUL for generations to come. All the years of sowing the words of truth upon the mind and heart of a young boy who grew to a young adult were not in vain. All the years he had gone to camp with the memories of the Word of Truth being embedded into the hearts of young boys growing into godly men were not in vain. With renewed insight I left for my week at Deerfoot embracing the week that lay ahead. The LORD had shed a light on what was to become a week filled with joy.

The week was in fact beyond what I could have envisioned. Though there were moments that moved me to tears as I listened to the songs, saw the skits, heard the testimonies of the campers and shared in the moments that make Deerfoot the amazing wilderness experience it is for young boys, there was much joy. I read and re-read that text of Scripture and thought through the promise of the offspring's offspring. We serve a LORD and King who does not lie and who by the blood of His Son cemented a covenant upon the hearts of His people. ***Nothing*** can erase that inscribed covenant that is written upon the heart by the Spirit of the living God. We turn from Him, grieve His Spirit, are stubborn and stiff-necked but He is the FAITHFUL covenant keeper who waits for His prodigals to come home.

7

JEWELS OF GRACE:
Standing On The Promises

So many years have come and gone since that summer long ago. Life has moved on and the journey continues. The LORD of Glory still in control who has taught His daughter continually over these years one step at a time. He has allowed this child to grow, becoming the matured woman He desires me to be in the fullness of Jesus Christ. The process was not an easy one; to be a child of the King and become who He wants us to be involves pain.

The phenomenon of pain and suffering continues through the ages. The questions asked through pain and suffering are asked by every person, some verbally, some silently. How the questions are answered will either cause some to grow in relationship to the LORD or for others it will be the wedge which severs relationship with Him. The questions are not new and always resigned to the integrity of His goodness, question His love, or doubt His protection and provision. Why would a God who loves His creation and desires its best allow such suffering and pain? How can God be good and send good people to hell or allow bad things to happen to good people? What kind of a God is that anyway?

Are these questions justified? Can a Christian who knows the truth of Scripture and holds fast the truth of a Sovereign God walk away with this understanding? Did the sages of old believe these things, can we? We are no different in the struggles of this life or the pain and sorrows it offers. To be ignorant to it or to believe the lies of the current day 'false prophets' leaves us vulnerable, much like Eve in the garden choosing her own wisdom over God's. Nothing from His hand is without meaning or void of purpose, each detail of our lives is to be crafted into a Jewel of Grace for His kingdom.

Through all the pain of Job, his loses, his suffering, his doubting, his questions, his voice raised in accusations, Job had a clear understanding from where the circumstances of the depth of his suffering came. A verse known by many found in Job 2:10 says, "Shall we accept good from God and not accept adversity?" Great, got it, all clear. We have a lid on pain and suffering. We can move on to the next topic that has the potential to shatter our lives.

However, if we search a little more the issue of a good God allowing very hard and sometimes seemingly cruel situations tests the core of our souls as it did Job's. Chapter 5 declares the LORD as the One who inflicts pain and gives relief. In Chapter 7 Job speaks of the "anguish of my spirit, and complains about the bitterness of my soul" (vs.11). In that same chapter the "righteous" Job laments and brazenly asks the LORD, "What have I done to You, O watcher of men? Why have you set me as Your target?" And if his suffering was not enough, God allowed his three close friends to show up on the scene and offer their comforting words! In Job 16 he calls them miserable comforters. In all his anguish he understands, "God has delivered me to the ungodly and turned me over to the hands of the wicked." (Job 16:11) Through all the pain and suffering Job endured his claim to innocence remained steadfast. His prayers were "pure" and there was no "violence in his hands."

This Sovereign LORD who loved Job is also the LORD who loves us and provides us with comfort that comes from the Grace of His promises. REALLY?? How can this be true? We find in so many places in this story the laments of pain and suffering coming from a man who was blameless and without cause. Yet, it was Job's conviction about the reality of God which filled him with relentless dependence and affirmation of His God. Job's pain was not without purpose and neither is mine or yours. In his journey Job learned of His God. His moment of truth, of profound revelation recorded for all humanity to read in Job, Chapter 42:3, "Therefore, I have uttered what I did not understand, things too wonderful for me, which I did not know." Job's moment of resolution, his greatest ah ha moment came through a process that contained a time of great anguish, pain and suffering. We are not exempt; we too will be given the same journey though not asked for, just like Job, and we will like Job, "pour out our tears to God." (Job 16:20)

Turn the pages of the Scripture to the weeping prophet, Jeremiah and read his laments in Chapter 3 of Lamentations. Right out of the gate in verse one, Jeremiah makes no qualm in allowing the reader to understand his "affliction" comes from the rod of Yahweh's wrath. Verse 3, "Surely against me He has turned His Hand," verse 4, "He has caused my flesh and my skin to waste away," verse 8, "Even when I cry out and call for help, He shuts out my prayer." Verse after verse filled with anguish from this prophet the LORD had formed in the womb and appointed to be the prophet to the nations! In all his pain He knew his LORD, the One he could hope in and proclaim, *"The LORD's lovingkindness indeed never ceases... Great is thy **FAITHFULNESS**."* (Lamentations 3:22 & 23, italics and bold mine).

Jesus becomes our greatest example and our greatest challenge. No one before Him or after Him will ever endure His suffering and shame. On a tree He alone bore the wrath of sin. His outstretched arms embraced the penalty of hell. No one who trusts in Him will ever need to go to that extreme. No one will endure the agony of that moment in history where sin was made a public display. Where satan and the powers of darkness were triumphantly destroyed for all humanity to see. God's hostility towards sin, all the debt of our sin in one agonizing moment was cancelled, forever done. That is Amazing Grace and we enter into relationship with the living God because of Christ.

The pages of history tell the story of those who like Christ bear His image in taking up the Cross of suffering and shame. "For to you it has been granted, for Christ's sake, not only to believe in him, but also to suffer for his sake…" (Philippians 1:29) And in the words of Jesus Himself, "He who does not pick up his cross and follow after Me is not worthy of Me." (Matthew 10:38)

Like so many before me and like so many that will come after, who struggle with the dilemma of suffering, with all its doubts and raised fists, I, too, come to the resolution that my Sovereign LORD and KING is a God of goodness, and His provision and mercies are new every day. I know my Redeemer lives. As I go through this journey I learn suffering, pain and sorrow comes as the result of a broken humanity, not a God void of love, goodness, provision or protection for me.

In the gift of faith, pain and suffering provide a tender Jewel of Grace. It is not a one-time moment, but a journey. They are the tremendous Jewels of Grace the LORD used in my life to allow me to be shaped into the image of the One who gave me so much. The magnitude of suffering provides victory. Though here in a world of quick fixes the very thought is repulsive. Pain transforms our lives, stretches us to levels we never could have understood. It is a pathway of our best growth, our greatest discoveries and our deepest possession of continued dependence on our LORD. In the anguish of our suffering and pain we, like Abraham, can offer worship in the Isaac we are called to lay down and offer as our sacrifice.

Every Christian is quick to quote Romans 8:28. A verse I love is Isaiah 48:10, "I have refined you," sounds wonderful; I like the illustration of being refined. I like knowing all things work together for good too, but a closer look at these verses gives me the process, "but not as silver; I have tested you in the *furnace of affliction.*" (italics mine). Romans 8:29 again gives me the process that working together for good must take; it is "to be conformed to the image of Christ." The LORD has revealed that process in the life of my Savior. One filled with loneliness, one filled with a *kiss* of betrayal from a *friend*, one filled with the denial of a *friend* closest to Him, one filled with abandonment of His *friends*, one filled with being acquainted with sorrow and grief and one filled with men and woman who despised and rejected Him both then and now, to arms stretched open in agony on a tree. Who of us would be willing to sign on the dotted line to demonstrate such an act of love for such a thankless world as ours?

For a season I stopped writing this book. I had no understanding why. I sought the LORD and had no answer for the reason. I asked Him to search my heart. I wanted to write but could not. I shared my feelings with a friend. She encouraged me, "When the LORD sees fit you will write again." In time I came to understand my dilemma rested in how to complete the writing of this book. The LORD was teaching me so much during my quiet time away from writing. None of it, I felt, dealt with completing the writing of this book.

One day, as I thought about it again, a verse the LORD had given me in those first weeks after my son walked away came to my mind. "Be anxious for nothing, but in everything by prayer and supplication with thanksgiving let your requests be made known to God. And the *peace of God*, which surpasses all *comprehension*, shall guard your hearts and your minds in Christ Jesus." Philippians 4:6-7 (italics and bold mine). The New Living Translation says it this way: *"Then you will experience God's peace, which exceeds anything we can understand."*

It was my Rhema from the LORD, what I had been searching for. I had come full circle! My Yahweh was giving to His daughter the very promise He had given me so many years ago. How many times had I read this verse since that painful time so long ago, never making the connection? This was what the LORD had wanted me to understand, what He had been teaching me throughout all the years. With every surrender He offered me something greater—Peace. In the greatest moments of pain, of suffering we can have peace. I have written in my Bible a peace that makes no sense.

In Hebrew the word for peace is shalom. The deepest sense of the meaning of shalom is to have a deep inner contentment, a sense of joy that all things are well because the God of tranquility abides within me. That is shalom. The LORD understood in this journey none of us would be left untouched or exempt from pain, but He would offer us shalom, His abiding presence to give us inner peace and stability through the darkest moments of life.

For those of us who walk through this journey together, who love a prodigal with all our hearts and see their lives lived away from a God who loves them so much we are left with a hollow in our heart and pain. One of the greatest gifts we are given is a child, and as 3 John 4 says, "I have no greater joy than this, to hear of my children walking in the truth." The reality of that joy though is not for all, our children fall away and leave the faith they once embraced.

As I wait through these years on the LORD in prayerful expectancy, I have learned that my greatest moments of pain have become my greatest Jewels of Grace. I have learned again and again, He hears me, He is attentive to my cries and He turns His ear towards me. He is my loving Abba, who takes every tear I cry and puts them in a bottle held in His hands of Grace and knows why each was shed.

The High Priest of heaven took on the face of humanity and entered a world filled with pain and sorrow. He allowed Himself to be humiliated for me so I could be identified with Him and bear His image and learn that each step of my journey on this earth is with the purpose to be conformed to the One who gave Himself for me.

He has allowed me to be in the wilderness of pain and spoken tenderly words of comfort to His daughter time and time again. He has taught me to pray from the anguish deep within my soul. He has taught me to trust Him when there is only silence, when the answers seem so out of reach to the questions I cannot bear or understand and all around appears hopeless. He has held his daughter's heart a million times in His loving hands and shown me His promises are "yea and amen." He has exposed my sinful rebellion again-and-again and remained my FAITHFUL I AM. His unfailing love for me poured out page after page and verse after verse in His Word of Truth. I have learned, not once has He failed me and never will He. He is the LORD who will lead me, sustain me and guide me even until death. And yes, I believe it was this specific journey that the LORD used to refine me and teach me that no matter where His Hand allows me to go, I will be like Habakkuk and proclaim, "I will exult in the LORD, I will rejoice in the God of my salvation." (Hab. 3:18) He is my LORD and my strength. I can believe Him and trust Him even when I don't understand the whys and even when I have no clue as to the outcome. There is no crown without a cross.

A pen silenced by a LORD who had a plan for His daughter. There was yet another wilderness He needed to lead me through. I needed to learn He offered me peace. Although the moments of sadness and tears would come again, there would be the peace He offered me as His guiding Hand held mine engraven within His for all eternity. This LORD over all would bring an inner peace not of this world, not afforded by the remedies of man but the Peace of an Everlasting LORD of Lords and KING of Kings. I know the triumph of the Cross, the inner tranquility, which says it is well with my soul.

My son is one of the most precious gifts I have been given. As his mother I will never stop praying to the LORD I know is able. **NOTHING** is too difficult for my God. I am the woman of Luke 18, standing, knocking forever on the doors of heaven for my prodigal to come home, confident in the outcome. The prayers are now deeper, with prayer concerns involving so much more. In all of this I have been embraced by my loving Father, who hears me, turning His ear towards me, putting my tears into His Bottle of Grace; Amazing wonderful Grace, and then surrounds my soul with peace, a peace that makes no sense.

To God be the Glory!

ABOUT THE AUTHOR

Mari Madonna was born on Long Island, N.Y., where she raised her only son as a single mother. She retired in 2010 from her work as an RN in the Emergency Room of a Level One trauma center.

In 2001 she studied Old Testament Theology at Alliance Theological Seminary in Nyack, N.Y. In 2004 Stand In The Gap began, which is an intercessory prayer ministry for the prodigals of loved ones.

Mari now lives in Pennsylvania with her Mother. Her son and his family live close to her. She enjoys caring for her two granddaughters, who are the joy of her life. She continues to work part-time as a nurse.

Made in the USA
Middletown, DE
24 August 2022